## THIS BOOK BELONGS TO

......................................

......................................

First published in Great Britain in 1994
by Methuen Children's Books
an imprint of Reed Children's Books
Michelin House, 81 Fulham Road, London SW3 6RB
and Auckland, Melbourne, Singapore and Toronto
This presentation copyright © 1994 Reed International Books Limited
Illustrations by Alfred Bestall copyright © 1949, 1969 Express Newspapers Limited
Illustrations by John Harrold copyright © 1991, 1992, 1993 Express Newspapers plc
Rupert Characters TM & © 1994 Express Newspapers plc
Licensed by Nelvana Marketing Inc.,
U.K. representatives: Abbey Home Entertainment Licensing

ISBN 0 416 18986 5

Produced by Mandarin

Printed and bound in Hong Kong

# RUPERT™
## DIARY 1995

Methuen

# PERSONAL FILE

Name ........................................................

Address ...................................................

...............................................................

Telephone (home)....................................

Telephone (work)...................................

National Insurance number ....................

Passport number.....................................

Driving licence number ..........................

Car registration.......................................

AA/RAC Membership number...................

Car insurance number .............................

National Health number..........................

Blood group .............................................

Any known allergies.................................

Doctor ........................      Dentist .........................

Address .......................      Address .......................

.....................................      .....................................

.....................................      .....................................

Telephone ....................      Telephone ....................

Emergency credit card      Bank account number

phone numbers ...............

.....................................      Bank address...................

In emergency contact:......      .....................................

.....................................      .....................................

.....................................      Telephone ....................

# *TELEPHONE NUMBERS*

| | |
|---|---|
| HOME . . . . . . . . . . . . . . . . . . . | RAILWAY STATION . . . . . . . . . . |
| WORK . . . . . . . . . . . . . . . . . . . | . . . . . . . . . . . . . . . . . . . . . . . . . . . . . . |
| . . . . . . . . . . . . . . . . . . . . . . . . . . | CINEMA . . . . . . . . . . . . . . . . . . . |
| SCHOOL. . . . . . . . . . . . . . . . . . | . . . . . . . . . . . . . . . . . . . . . . . . . . . . . . |
| DOCTOR . . . . . . . . . . . . . . . . . | TAXI . . . . . . . . . . . . . . . . . . . . . . |
| DENTIST . . . . . . . . . . . . . . . . . | . . . . . . . . . . . . . . . . . . . . . . . . . . . . . . |
| BANK . . . . . . . . . . . . . . . . . . . | PLUMBER . . . . . . . . . . . . . . . . . . |
| POLICE STATION. . . . . . . . . . . | ELECTRICIAN . . . . . . . . . . . . . . . |
| . . . . . . . . . . . . . . . . . . . . . . . . . . | GAS . . . . . . . . . . . . . . . . . . . . . . . |
| LOCAL AUTHORITY. . . . . . . . | TELEPHONE ENGINEER. . . . . . . |
| . . . . . . . . . . . . . . . . . . . . . . . . . . | . . . . . . . . . . . . . . . . . . . . . . . . . . . . . . |
| NEIGHBOURS. . . . . . . . . . . . . . | OTHER . . . . . . . . . . . . . . . . . . . . |
| . . . . . . . . . . . . . . . . . . . . . . . . . . | . . . . . . . . . . . . . . . . . . . . . . . . . . . . . . |
| . . . . . . . . . . . . . . . . . . . . . . . . . . | . . . . . . . . . . . . . . . . . . . . . . . . . . . . . . |

# CALENDARS

## 1994

### JANUARY
| | | | | | | |
|---|---|---|---|---|---|---|
| Monday | . | 3 | 10 | 17 | 24 | 31 |
| Tuesday | . | 4 | 11 | 18 | 25 | . |
| Wednesday | . | 5 | 12 | 19 | 26 | . |
| Thursday | . | 6 | 13 | 20 | 27 | . |
| Friday | . | 7 | 14 | 21 | 28 | . |
| Saturday | 1 | 8 | 15 | 22 | 29 | . |
| Sunday | 2 | 9 | 16 | 23 | 30 | . |

### FEBRUARY
| | | | | | | |
|---|---|---|---|---|---|---|
| Monday | . | 7 | 14 | 21 | 28 | . |
| Tuesday | 1 | 8 | 15 | 22 | . | . |
| Wednesday | 2 | 9 | 16 | 23 | . | . |
| Thursday | 3 | 10 | 17 | 24 | . | . |
| Friday | 4 | 11 | 18 | 25 | . | . |
| Saturday | 5 | 12 | 19 | 26 | . | . |
| Sunday | 6 | 13 | 20 | 27 | . | . |

### MARCH
| | | | | | | |
|---|---|---|---|---|---|---|
| Monday | . | 7 | 14 | 21 | 28 | . |
| Tuesday | 1 | 8 | 15 | 22 | 29 | . |
| Wednesday | 2 | 9 | 16 | 23 | 30 | . |
| Thursday | 3 | 10 | 17 | 24 | 31 | . |
| Friday | 4 | 11 | 18 | 25 | . | . |
| Saturday | 5 | 12 | 19 | 26 | . | . |
| Sunday | 6 | 13 | 20 | 27 | . | . |

### APRIL
| | | | | | | |
|---|---|---|---|---|---|---|
| Monday | . | 4 | 11 | 18 | 25 | . |
| Tuesday | . | 5 | 12 | 19 | 26 | . |
| Wednesday | . | 6 | 13 | 20 | 27 | . |
| Thursday | . | 7 | 14 | 21 | 28 | . |
| Friday | 1 | 8 | 15 | 22 | 29 | . |
| Saturday | 2 | 9 | 16 | 23 | 30 | . |
| Sunday | 3 | 10 | 17 | 24 | . | . |

### MAY
| | | | | | | |
|---|---|---|---|---|---|---|
| Monday | . | 2 | 9 | 16 | 23 | 30 |
| Tuesday | . | 3 | 10 | 17 | 24 | 31 |
| Wednesday | . | 4 | 11 | 18 | 25 | . |
| Thursday | . | 5 | 12 | 19 | 26 | . |
| Friday | . | 6 | 13 | 20 | 27 | . |
| Saturday | . | 7 | 14 | 21 | 28 | . |
| Sunday | 1 | 8 | 15 | 22 | 29 | . |

### JUNE
| | | | | | | |
|---|---|---|---|---|---|---|
| Monday | . | 6 | 13 | 20 | 27 | . |
| Tuesday | . | 7 | 14 | 21 | 28 | . |
| Wednesday | 1 | 8 | 15 | 22 | 29 | . |
| Thursday | 2 | 9 | 16 | 23 | 30 | . |
| Friday | 3 | 10 | 17 | 24 | . | . |
| Saturday | 4 | 11 | 18 | 25 | . | . |
| Sunday | 5 | 12 | 19 | 26 | . | . |

### JULY
| | | | | | | |
|---|---|---|---|---|---|---|
| Monday | . | 4 | 11 | 18 | 25 | . |
| Tuesday | . | 5 | 12 | 19 | 26 | . |
| Wednesday | . | 6 | 13 | 20 | 27 | . |
| Thursday | . | 7 | 14 | 21 | 28 | . |
| Friday | 1 | 8 | 15 | 22 | 29 | . |
| Saturday | 2 | 9 | 16 | 23 | 30 | . |
| Sunday | 3 | 10 | 17 | 24 | 31 | . |

### AUGUST
| | | | | | | |
|---|---|---|---|---|---|---|
| Monday | 1 | 8 | 15 | 22 | 29 | . |
| Tuesday | 2 | 9 | 16 | 23 | 30 | . |
| Wednesday | 3 | 10 | 17 | 24 | 31 | . |
| Thursday | 4 | 11 | 18 | 25 | . | . |
| Friday | 5 | 12 | 19 | 26 | . | . |
| Saturday | 6 | 13 | 20 | 27 | . | . |
| Sunday | 7 | 14 | 21 | 28 | . | . |

### SEPTEMBER
| | | | | | | |
|---|---|---|---|---|---|---|
| Monday | . | 5 | 12 | 19 | 26 | . |
| Tuesday | . | 6 | 13 | 20 | 27 | . |
| Wednesday | . | 7 | 14 | 21 | 28 | . |
| Thursday | 1 | 8 | 15 | 22 | 29 | . |
| Friday | 2 | 9 | 16 | 23 | 30 | . |
| Saturday | 3 | 10 | 17 | 24 | . | . |
| Sunday | 4 | 11 | 18 | 25 | . | . |

### OCTOBER
| | | | | | | |
|---|---|---|---|---|---|---|
| Monday | . | 3 | 10 | 17 | 24 | 31 |
| Tuesday | . | 4 | 11 | 18 | 25 | . |
| Wednesday | . | 5 | 12 | 19 | 26 | . |
| Thursday | . | 6 | 13 | 20 | 27 | . |
| Friday | . | 7 | 14 | 21 | 28 | . |
| Saturday | 1 | 8 | 15 | 22 | 29 | . |
| Sunday | 2 | 9 | 16 | 23 | 30 | . |

### NOVEMBER
| | | | | | | |
|---|---|---|---|---|---|---|
| Monday | . | 7 | 14 | 21 | 28 | . |
| Tuesday | 1 | 8 | 15 | 22 | 29 | . |
| Wednesday | 2 | 9 | 16 | 23 | 30 | . |
| Thursday | 3 | 10 | 17 | 24 | . | . |
| Friday | 4 | 11 | 18 | 25 | . | . |
| Saturday | 5 | 12 | 19 | 26 | . | . |
| Sunday | 6 | 13 | 20 | 27 | . | . |

### DECEMBER
| | | | | | | |
|---|---|---|---|---|---|---|
| Monday | . | 5 | 12 | 19 | 26 | . |
| Tuesday | . | 6 | 13 | 20 | 27 | . |
| Wednesday | . | 7 | 14 | 21 | 28 | . |
| Thursday | 1 | 8 | 15 | 22 | 29 | . |
| Friday | 2 | 9 | 16 | 23 | 30 | . |
| Saturday | 3 | 10 | 17 | 24 | 31 | . |
| Sunday | 4 | 11 | 18 | 25 | . | . |

## 1995

### JANUARY
| | | | | | |
|---|---|---|---|---|---|
| Monday | . | 2 | 9 | 16 | 23 |
| Tuesday | . | 3 | 10 | 17 | 24 |
| Wednesday | . | 4 | 11 | 18 | 25 |
| Thursday | . | 5 | 12 | 19 | 26 |
| Friday | . | 6 | 13 | 20 | 27 |
| Saturday | . | 7 | 14 | 21 | 28 |
| Sunday | 1 | 8 | 15 | 22 | 29 |

### FEBRUARY
| | | | | | |
|---|---|---|---|---|---|
| Monday | . | 6 | 13 | 20 | 27 |
| Tuesday | . | 7 | 14 | 21 | 28 |
| Wednesday | 1 | 8 | 15 | 22 | . |
| Thursday | 2 | 9 | 16 | 23 | . |
| Friday | 3 | 10 | 17 | 24 | . |
| Saturday | 4 | 11 | 18 | 25 | . |
| Sunday | 5 | 12 | 19 | 26 | . |

### MARCH
| | | | | | |
|---|---|---|---|---|---|
| Monday | . | 6 | 13 | 20 | 27 |
| Tuesday | . | 7 | 14 | 21 | 28 |
| Wednesday | 1 | 8 | 15 | 22 | 29 |
| Thursday | 2 | 9 | 16 | 23 | 30 |
| Friday | 3 | 10 | 17 | 24 | 31 |
| Saturday | 4 | 11 | 18 | 25 | . |
| Sunday | 5 | 12 | 19 | 26 | . |

### APRIL
| | | | | | |
|---|---|---|---|---|---|
| Monday | . | 3 | 10 | 17 | 24 |
| Tuesday | . | 4 | 11 | 18 | 25 |
| Wednesday | . | 5 | 12 | 19 | 26 |
| Thursday | . | 6 | 13 | 20 | 27 |
| Friday | . | 7 | 14 | 21 | 28 |
| Saturday | 1 | 8 | 15 | 22 | 29 |
| Sunday | 2 | 9 | 16 | 23 | 30 |

### MAY
| | | | | | |
|---|---|---|---|---|---|
| Monday | 1 | 8 | 15 | 22 | 29 |
| Tuesday | 2 | 9 | 16 | 23 | 30 |
| Wednesday | 3 | 10 | 17 | 24 | 31 |
| Thursday | 4 | 11 | 18 | 25 | . |
| Friday | 5 | 12 | 19 | 26 | . |
| Saturday | 6 | 13 | 20 | 27 | . |
| Sunday | 7 | 14 | 21 | 28 | . |

### JUNE
| | | | | | |
|---|---|---|---|---|---|
| Monday | . | 5 | 12 | 19 | 26 |
| Tuesday | . | 6 | 13 | 20 | 27 |
| Wednesday | . | 7 | 14 | 21 | 28 |
| Thursday | 1 | 8 | 15 | 22 | 29 |
| Friday | 2 | 9 | 16 | 23 | 30 |
| Saturday | 3 | 10 | 17 | 24 | . |
| Sunday | 4 | 11 | 18 | 25 | . |

# CALENDARS

| LY | | | | | | |
|---|---|---|---|---|---|---|
| onday | . | 3 | 10 | 17 | 24 | 31 |
| esday | . | 4 | 11 | 18 | 25 | . |
| ednesday | . | 5 | 12 | 19 | 26 | . |
| ursday | . | 6 | 13 | 20 | 27 | . |
| iday | . | 7 | 14 | 21 | 28 | . |
| turday | 1 | 8 | 15 | 22 | 29 | . |
| nday | 2 | 9 | 16 | 23 | 30 | . |

| UGUST | | | | | | |
|---|---|---|---|---|---|---|
| onday | . | 7 | 14 | 21 | 28 | . |
| esday | 1 | 8 | 15 | 22 | 29 | . |
| ednesday | 2 | 9 | 16 | 23 | 30 | . |
| ursday | 3 | 10 | 17 | 24 | 31 | . |
| iday | 4 | 11 | 18 | 25 | . | . |
| turday | 5 | 12 | 19 | 26 | . | . |
| nday | 6 | 13 | 20 | 27 | . | . |

| PTEMBER | | | | | | |
|---|---|---|---|---|---|---|
| onday | . | 4 | 11 | 18 | 25 | . |
| esday | . | 5 | 12 | 19 | 26 | . |
| ednesday | . | 6 | 13 | 20 | 27 | . |
| ursday | . | 7 | 14 | 21 | 28 | . |
| iday | 1 | 8 | 15 | 22 | 29 | . |
| turday | 2 | 9 | 16 | 23 | 30 | . |
| nday | 3 | 10 | 17 | 24 | . | . |

| CTOBER | | | | | | |
|---|---|---|---|---|---|---|
| onday | . | 2 | 9 | 16 | 23 | 30 |
| uesday | . | 3 | 10 | 17 | 24 | 31 |
| ednesday | . | 4 | 11 | 18 | 25 | . |
| hursday | . | 5 | 12 | 19 | 26 | . |
| riday | . | 6 | 13 | 20 | 27 | . |
| aturday | . | 7 | 14 | 21 | 28 | . |
| unday | 1 | 8 | 15 | 22 | 29 | . |

| OVEMBER | | | | | | |
|---|---|---|---|---|---|---|
| onday | . | 6 | 13 | 20 | 27 | . |
| uesday | . | 7 | 14 | 21 | 28 | . |
| Vednesday | 1 | 8 | 15 | 22 | 29 | . |
| hursday | 2 | 9 | 16 | 23 | 30 | . |
| riday | 3 | 10 | 17 | 24 | . | . |
| aturday | 4 | 11 | 18 | 25 | . | . |
| unday | 5 | 12 | 19 | 26 | . | . |

| ECEMBER | | | | | | |
|---|---|---|---|---|---|---|
| Monday | . | 4 | 11 | 18 | 25 | . |
| uesday | . | 5 | 12 | 19 | 26 | . |
| Vednesday | . | 6 | 13 | 20 | 27 | . |
| hursday | . | 7 | 14 | 21 | 28 | . |
| riday | 1 | 8 | 15 | 22 | 29 | . |
| aturday | 2 | 9 | 16 | 23 | 30 | . |
| unday | 3 | 10 | 17 | 24 | 31 | . |

## 1996

| JANUARY | | | | | | |
|---|---|---|---|---|---|---|
| Monday | 1 | 8 | 15 | 22 | 29 | . |
| Tuesday | 2 | 9 | 16 | 23 | 30 | . |
| Wednesday | 3 | 10 | 17 | 24 | 31 | . |
| Thursday | 4 | 11 | 18 | 25 | . | . |
| Friday | 5 | 12 | 19 | 26 | . | . |
| Saturday | 6 | 13 | 20 | 27 | . | . |
| Sunday | 7 | 14 | 21 | 28 | . | . |

| FEBRUARY | | | | | | |
|---|---|---|---|---|---|---|
| Monday | . | 5 | 12 | 19 | 26 | . |
| Tuesday | . | 6 | 13 | 20 | 27 | . |
| Wednesday | . | 7 | 14 | 21 | 28 | . |
| Thursday | 1 | 8 | 15 | 22 | 29 | . |
| Friday | 2 | 9 | 16 | 23 | . | . |
| Saturday | 3 | 10 | 17 | 24 | . | . |
| Sunday | 4 | 11 | 18 | 25 | . | . |

| MARCH | | | | | | |
|---|---|---|---|---|---|---|
| Monday | . | 4 | 11 | 18 | 25 | . |
| Tuesday | . | 5 | 12 | 19 | 26 | . |
| Wednesday | . | 6 | 13 | 20 | 27 | . |
| Thursday | . | 7 | 14 | 21 | 28 | . |
| Friday | 1 | 8 | 15 | 22 | 29 | . |
| Saturday | 2 | 9 | 16 | 23 | 30 | . |
| Sunday | 3 | 10 | 17 | 24 | 31 | . |

| APRIL | | | | | | |
|---|---|---|---|---|---|---|
| Monday | 1 | 8 | 15 | 22 | 29 | . |
| Tuesday | 2 | 9 | 16 | 23 | 30 | . |
| Wednesday | 3 | 10 | 17 | 24 | . | . |
| Thursday | 4 | 11 | 18 | 25 | . | . |
| Friday | 5 | 12 | 19 | 26 | . | . |
| Saturday | 6 | 13 | 20 | 27 | . | . |
| Sunday | 7 | 14 | 21 | 28 | . | . |

| MAY | | | | | | |
|---|---|---|---|---|---|---|
| Monday | . | 6 | 13 | 20 | 27 | . |
| Tuesday | . | 7 | 14 | 21 | 28 | . |
| Wednesday | 1 | 8 | 15 | 22 | 29 | . |
| Thursday | 2 | 9 | 16 | 23 | 30 | . |
| Friday | 3 | 10 | 17 | 24 | 31 | . |
| Saturday | 4 | 11 | 18 | 25 | . | . |
| Sunday | 5 | 12 | 19 | 26 | . | . |

| JUNE | | | | | | |
|---|---|---|---|---|---|---|
| Monday | . | 3 | 10 | 17 | 24 | . |
| Tuesday | . | 4 | 11 | 18 | 25 | . |
| Wednesday | . | 5 | 12 | 19 | 26 | . |
| Thursday | . | 6 | 13 | 20 | 27 | . |
| Friday | . | 7 | 14 | 21 | 28 | . |
| Saturday | 1 | 8 | 15 | 22 | 29 | . |
| Sunday | 2 | 9 | 16 | 23 | 30 | . |

| JULY | | | | | | |
|---|---|---|---|---|---|---|
| Monday | 1 | 8 | 15 | 22 | 29 | . |
| Tuesday | 2 | 9 | 16 | 23 | 30 | . |
| Wednesday | 3 | 10 | 17 | 24 | 31 | . |
| Thursday | 4 | 11 | 18 | 25 | . | . |
| Friday | 5 | 12 | 19 | 26 | . | . |
| Saturday | 6 | 13 | 20 | 27 | . | . |
| Sunday | 7 | 14 | 21 | 28 | . | . |

| AUGUST | | | | | | |
|---|---|---|---|---|---|---|
| Monday | . | 5 | 12 | 19 | 26 | . |
| Tuesday | . | 6 | 13 | 20 | 27 | . |
| Wednesday | . | 7 | 14 | 21 | 28 | . |
| Thursday | 1 | 8 | 15 | 22 | 29 | . |
| Friday | 2 | 9 | 16 | 23 | 30 | . |
| Saturday | 3 | 10 | 17 | 24 | 31 | . |
| Sunday | 4 | 11 | 18 | 25 | . | . |

| SEPTEMBER | | | | | | |
|---|---|---|---|---|---|---|
| Monday | . | 2 | 9 | 16 | 23 | 30 |
| Tuesday | . | 3 | 10 | 17 | 24 | . |
| Wednesday | . | 4 | 11 | 18 | 25 | . |
| Thursday | . | 5 | 12 | 19 | 26 | . |
| Friday | . | 6 | 13 | 20 | 27 | . |
| Saturday | . | 7 | 14 | 21 | 28 | . |
| Sunday | 1 | 8 | 15 | 22 | 29 | . |

| OCTOBER | | | | | | |
|---|---|---|---|---|---|---|
| Monday | . | 7 | 14 | 21 | 28 | . |
| Tuesday | 1 | 8 | 15 | 22 | 29 | . |
| Wednesday | 2 | 9 | 16 | 23 | 30 | . |
| Thursday | 3 | 10 | 17 | 24 | 31 | . |
| Friday | 4 | 11 | 18 | 25 | . | . |
| Saturday | 5 | 12 | 19 | 26 | . | . |
| Sunday | 6 | 13 | 20 | 27 | . | . |

| NOVEMBER | | | | | | |
|---|---|---|---|---|---|---|
| Monday | . | 4 | 11 | 18 | 25 | . |
| Tuesday | . | 5 | 12 | 19 | 26 | . |
| Wednesday | . | 6 | 13 | 20 | 27 | . |
| Thursday | . | 7 | 14 | 21 | 28 | . |
| Friday | 1 | 8 | 15 | 22 | 29 | . |
| Saturday | 2 | 9 | 16 | 23 | 30 | . |
| Sunday | 3 | 10 | 17 | 24 | . | . |

| DECEMBER | | | | | | |
|---|---|---|---|---|---|---|
| Monday | . | 2 | 9 | 16 | 23 | 30 |
| Tuesday | . | 3 | 10 | 17 | 24 | 31 |
| Wednesday | . | 4 | 11 | 18 | 25 | . |
| Thursday | . | 5 | 12 | 19 | 26 | . |
| Friday | . | 6 | 13 | 20 | 27 | . |
| Saturday | . | 7 | 14 | 21 | 28 | . |
| Sunday | 1 | 8 | 15 | 22 | 29 | . |

# NOTABLE DATES

| 1 | JANUARY | New Year's Day |
| 2 | JANUARY | Bank Holiday (UK and Rep. of Ireland) |
| 3 | JANUARY | Bank Holiday (Scotland) |
| 17 | MARCH | St Patrick's Day (Rep. of Ireland and N. Ireland) |
| 26 | MARCH | Mothers' Day |
| 14 | APRIL | Good Friday (Holiday UK and Rep. of Ireland) |
| 16 | APRIL | Easter Day |
| 17 | APRIL | Easter Monday (Rep. of Ireland and UK except Scotland) |
| 1 | MAY | Spring Bank Holiday (Scotland) |
| 8 | MAY | V.E. Day Celebration – Bank Holiday (UK) |
| 29 | MAY | Bank Holiday (UK) |
| 5 | JUNE | Holiday (Rep. of Ireland) |
| 18 | JUNE | Fathers' Day |
| 12 | JULY | Bank Holiday (N. Ireland) |
| 7 | AUGUST | Summer Bank Holiday (Scotland) |
| 7 | AUGUST | Holiday (Rep. of Ireland) |
| 28 | AUGUST | Summer Bank Holiday (UK except Scotland) |
| 30 | OCTOBER | Holiday (Rep. of Ireland) |
| 25 | DECEMBER | Christmas Day |
| 26 | DECEMBER | Boxing Day (UK) |
| 26 | DECEMBER | St Stephen's Day (Rep. of Ireland) |

# RELIGIOUS FESTIVALS

## CHRISTIAN AND WESTERN

| 6 | JANUARY | Epiphany |
|---|---------|----------|
| 1 | MARCH | Ash Wednesday |
| 9 | APRIL | Palm Sunday |
| 14 | APRIL | Good Friday |
| 16 | APRIL | Easter Day |
| 23 | APRIL | Low Sunday |
| 21 | MAY | Rogation Sunday |
| 25 | MAY | Ascension Day – Holy Thursday |
| 4 | JUNE | Whit Sunday – Pentecost |
| 11 | JUNE | Trinity Sunday |
| 15 | JUNE | Corpus Christi |
| 15 | AUGUST | Assumption |
| 1 | NOVEMBER | All Saints Day |
| 3 | DECEMBER | First Sunday in Advent |
| 25 | DECEMBER | Christmas Day |

## JEWISH

| 15 | APRIL | Passover, First day of (Pesach) |
|---|---------|----------|
| 4 | JUNE | Feast of Weeks (Shavuot) |
| 25 | SEPTEMBER | Jewish New Year (5756) |
| 4 | OCTOBER | Day of Atonement (Yom Kippur) |
| 9 | OCTOBER | Tabernacles, First day of (Succoth) |
| 18 | DECEMBER | Chanukah |

## MUSLIM

| 1 | FEBRUARY | Ramadan begins |
|---|---------|----------|
| 3 | MARCH | Id-ul-Fitr |
| 10 | MAY | Id-ul-Adha |
| 31 | MAY | Islamic New Year (1416) |

# BIRTHDAYS

NAME . . . . . . . . . . . . . . . . .

BIRTHDAY . . . . . . . . . . . . .

NAME . . . . . . . . . . . . . . . . .

BIRTHDAY . . . . . . . . . . . . .

NAME . . . . . . . . . . . . . . . . .

BIRTHDAY . . . . . . . . . . . . .

NAME . . . . . . . . . . . . . . . . .

BIRTHDAY . . . . . . . . . . . . .

NAME . . . . . . . . . . . . . . . . .

BIRTHDAY . . . . . . . . . . . . .

NAME . . . . . . . . . . . . . . . . .

BIRTHDAY . . . . . . . . . . . . .

NAME . . . . . . . . . . . . . . . . .

BIRTHDAY . . . . . . . . . . . . .

NAME . . . . . . . . . . . . . . . . .

BIRTHDAY . . . . . . . . . . . . .

NAME . . . . . . . . . . . . . . . . .

BIRTHDAY . . . . . . . . . . . . .

NAME . . . . . . . . . . . . . . . . .

BIRTHDAY . . . . . . . . . . . . .

# SPECIAL OCCASIONS

OCCASION . . . . . . . . . . . . . .     OCCASION . . . . . . . . . . . . . .

DATE . . . . . . . . . . . . . . . .     DATE . . . . . . . . . . . . . . . .

OCCASION . . . . . . . . . . . . . .     OCCASION . . . . . . . . . . . . . .

DATE . . . . . . . . . . . . . . . .     DATE . . . . . . . . . . . . . . . .

OCCASION . . . . . . . . . . . . . .     OCCASION . . . . . . . . . . . . . .

DATE . . . . . . . . . . . . . . . .     DATE . . . . . . . . . . . . . . . .

OCCASION . . . . . . . . . . . . . .     OCCASION . . . . . . . . . . . . . .

DATE . . . . . . . . . . . . . . . .     DATE . . . . . . . . . . . . . . . .

OCCASION . . . . . . . . . . . . . .     OCCASION . . . . . . . . . . . . . .

DATE . . . . . . . . . . . . . . . .     DATE . . . . . . . . . . . . . . . .

# ADDRESSES

NAME . . . . . . . . . . . . . . . . . .

ADDRESS . . . . . . . . . . . . . . .

. . . . . . . . . . . . . . . . . . . . . . .

. . . . . . . . . . . . . . . . . . . . . . .

TELEPHONE . . . . . . . . . . . . .

NAME . . . . . . . . . . . . . . . . . .

ADDRESS . . . . . . . . . . . . . . .

. . . . . . . . . . . . . . . . . . . . . . .

. . . . . . . . . . . . . . . . . . . . . . .

TELEPHONE . . . . . . . . . . . . .

NAME . . . . . . . . . . . . . . . . . .

ADDRESS . . . . . . . . . . . . . . .

. . . . . . . . . . . . . . . . . . . . . . .

. . . . . . . . . . . . . . . . . . . . . . .

TELEPHONE . . . . . . . . . . . . .

NAME . . . . . . . . . . . . . . . . . .

ADDRESS . . . . . . . . . . . . . . .

. . . . . . . . . . . . . . . . . . . . . . .

. . . . . . . . . . . . . . . . . . . . . . .

TELEPHONE . . . . . . . . . . . . .

NAME . . . . . . . . . . . . . . . . . .

ADDRESS . . . . . . . . . . . . . . .

. . . . . . . . . . . . . . . . . . . . . . .

. . . . . . . . . . . . . . . . . . . . . . .

TELEPHONE . . . . . . . . . . . . .

NAME . . . . . . . . . . . . . . . . . .

ADDRESS . . . . . . . . . . . . . . .

. . . . . . . . . . . . . . . . . . . . . . .

. . . . . . . . . . . . . . . . . . . . . . .

TELEPHONE . . . . . . . . . . . . .

NAME . . . . . . . . . . . . . . . . . .

ADDRESS . . . . . . . . . . . . . . .

. . . . . . . . . . . . . . . . . . . . . . .

. . . . . . . . . . . . . . . . . . . . . . .

TELEPHONE . . . . . . . . . . . . .

NAME . . . . . . . . . . . . . . . . . .

ADDRESS . . . . . . . . . . . . . . .

. . . . . . . . . . . . . . . . . . . . . . .

. . . . . . . . . . . . . . . . . . . . . . .

TELEPHONE . . . . . . . . . . . . .

NAME . . . . . . . . . . . . . . . . . .

ADDRESS . . . . . . . . . . . . . . .

. . . . . . . . . . . . . . . . . . . . . . .

. . . . . . . . . . . . . . . . . . . . . . .

TELEPHONE . . . . . . . . . . . . .

NAME . . . . . . . . . . . . . . . . . .

ADDRESS . . . . . . . . . . . . . . .

. . . . . . . . . . . . . . . . . . . . . . .

. . . . . . . . . . . . . . . . . . . . . . .

TELEPHONE . . . . . . . . . . . . .

**RUPERT AND THE NATIONAL TRUST**

Rupert is the spokesbear for The National Trust, a registered charity which protects and maintains 230 properties and over 650,000 acres of countryside throughout England, Wales and Northern Ireland.

For more information about the Trust's work and Rupert events, contact:
The National Trust 071-222 9251

The National Trust for Scotland may be contacted on 031-226 5922.

# Freddy the fox

Use a 5" to 7" square of paper white on one side black (or brown) on the other. Always check your fold in the next diagram.

**1**
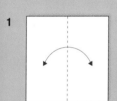

**2**
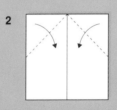

**3**
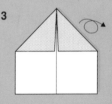

(1) White side up. Fold in half. Unfold. (2) Fold corners to centre line. (3) Turn model over - like turning a page in a book.

**4**
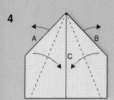

**5**
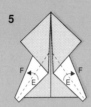

**6**
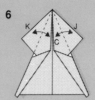

**7**
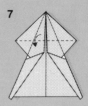

(4) Fold so edge 'A' lies along centre line 'C' let the flap underneath come out. Now do the same with 'B'. (5) Fold edge 'E' along 'F'.(both sides) (6) Fold edge 'J' along centre line 'C' and *open up* do the same with 'K' (7) Fold along dashed line.

**8**
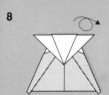

**9**

**10** **11**
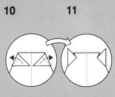

**12**
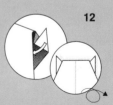

(8) Turn over like a page in a book. (9) Fold little flaps (ears) on dashed line. (10) Now fold the corners out again on dashed line. (11) This is the result now lift each ear and tuck *under* the top layer. (12) This is the ear being tucked under - do both now turn over.

(13) Fold up and crease on dashed line (about 1/3 of the way to the nose of the fox). (14) Hold each leg *below* the fold you made in step 13. Twist a little so your thumbs are on top and fingers below, now move the hands away from each other so the paper is tight - then bring the hands closer and Freddy will nod. (15) Move fingers together and then pull first one leg and then the other downwards, Freddy will put his head on one side.

**13** **15**

**14**

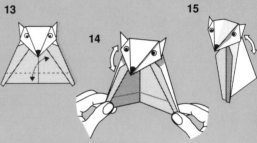

This design was created by John S Smith of the British Origami Society

**26** MONDAY

*Boxing Day (UK)*
*St Stephen's Day (Rep. of Ireland)*

**27** TUESDAY

*Bank Holiday (UK and Rep. of Ireland)*
*Holiday (Canada)*

**28** WEDNESDAY

**29** THURSDAY

*Then Jack and Rupert run to reach
Pong-Ping's to choose a reindeer each . . .*

**30** FRIDAY

**31** SATURDAY **1** SUNDAY

*New Year's Day*

# JANUARY

*"Hold tight now!" Rika warns as they*
*Take off, then calls, "Up and away!"*

**2**   MONDAY

*Bank Holiday (UK and Rep. of Ireland)*

**3**   TUESDAY

*Bank Holiday (Scotland)*

# JANUARY

**4**   WEDNESDAY

**5**   THURSDAY

**6**   FRIDAY

*Epiphany*

**7**   SATURDAY        **8**   SUNDAY

# JANUARY

**9**  MONDAY

**10**  TUESDAY

**11**  WEDNESDAY

**12**  THURSDAY

# JANUARY

*"We're almost there now!" Rupert cries*
*And points down to where Nutwood lies.*

**13** FRIDAY

**14** SATURDAY      **15** SUNDAY

# JANUARY

*The reindeer slowly circle round,*
*Then gently settle on the ground.*

**16**  MONDAY

**17**  TUESDAY

# JANUARY

**18** WEDNESDAY

**19** THURSDAY

**20** FRIDAY

**21** SATURDAY     **22** SUNDAY

# JANUARY

**23** MONDAY

**24** TUESDAY

**25** WEDNESDAY

**26** THURSDAY

*Soon Rika must be on her way,*
*"I'll come back next year, if I may . . . "*

---

**27**  FRIDAY

---

**28**  SATURDAY          **29**  SUNDAY

# JANUARY

*"A wooden sheep!" she laughs. "Bless me!*
*It looks as lifelike as can be . . . "*

**30** MONDAY

**31** TUESDAY

# FEBRUARY

**1** WEDNESDAY

*Ramadan begins*

**2** THURSDAY

**3** FRIDAY

**4** SATURDAY        **5** SUNDAY

# FEBRUARY

**6** MONDAY

**7** TUESDAY

**8** WEDNESDAY

**9** THURSDAY

# FEBRUARY

*The two pals crouch down, side by side,*
*And show him how they mean to hide.*

**10** FRIDAY

**11** SATURDAY    **12** SUNDAY

# FEBRUARY

*"The crooks!" gasps Bill. "So I was right,*
*They've come to steal more wool tonight!"*

**13** MONDAY

**14** TUESDAY

*St Valentine's Day*

# FEBRUARY

**15** WEDNESDAY

**16** THURSDAY

**17** FRIDAY

**18** SATURDAY  **19** SUNDAY

**20** MONDAY

**21** TUESDAY

**22** WEDNESDAY

**23** THURSDAY

# FEBRUARY

*Then Rupert slowly starts to creep*
*Towards the van, wheeling his sheep . . .*

**24** FRIDAY

**25** SATURDAY      **26** SUNDAY

# FEBRUARY

*As Rupert peers around the door*
*His pal lifts something from the straw . . .*

---

**27**  MONDAY

---

**28**  TUESDAY

# M A R C H

**1** WEDNESDAY

*St David's Day*
*Ash Wednesday*

**2** THURSDAY

**3** FRIDAY

**4** SATURDAY      **5** SUNDAY

# *M A R C H*

**6**    MONDAY

**7**    TUESDAY

**8**    WEDNESDAY

**9**    THURSDAY

# MARCH

*As Rupert speaks, the two pals see
The egg start moving suddenly . . .*

**10**  FRIDAY

**11**  SATURDAY      **12**  SUNDAY

# MARCH

*"Before the egg begins to crack
Let's see if we can put it back."*

---

**13** MONDAY

*Commonwealth Day*

---

**14** TUESDAY

# MARCH

**15** WEDNESDAY

**16** THURSDAY

**17** FRIDAY

*St Patrick's Day (Bank Holiday Rep. of Ireland and N. Ireland)*

**18** SATURDAY          **19** SUNDAY

# MARCH

**20** MONDAY

**21** TUESDAY

*Spring begins*

**22** WEDNESDAY

**23** THURSDAY

# MARCH

*"A baby ostrich! Goodness me!"*
*He smiles and strokes it tenderly.*

---

**24**  FRIDAY

---

**25**  SATURDAY

**26**  SUNDAY

*Mothers' Day*
*British Summer Time begins*

# M A R C H

*Inside the maze, a strange house lies*
*Which makes the two friends rub their eyes!*

---

**27**  MONDAY

---

**28**  TUESDAY

**29** WEDNESDAY

**30** THURSDAY

**31** FRIDAY

**1** SATURDAY     **2** SUNDAY

# APRIL

**3**   MONDAY

**4**   TUESDAY

**5**   WEDNESDAY

**6**   THURSDAY

# APRIL

*He rings the bell and straightaway*
*The flowers drench Willie with their spray!*

**7**   FRIDAY

**8**   SATURDAY    **9**   SUNDAY

*Palm Sunday*

# *APRIL*

*The pair climb up the stairs, but then*
*Find that they're going down again!*

**10**  MONDAY

**11**  TUESDAY

# APRIL

**12** WEDNESDAY

**13** THURSDAY

**14** FRIDAY

*Good Friday (Bank Holiday UK and Rep. of Ireland)*

**15** SATURDAY          **16** SUNDAY

*First day of Passover (Pesach)*                              *Easter Day*

# APRIL

**17** MONDAY

*Easter Monday (Bank Holiday Rep. of Ireland and UK except Scotland)*

**18** TUESDAY

**19** WEDNESDAY

**20** THURSDAY

# APRIL

*"Well done!" a voice calls. "You're my guests!*
*I hope you both enjoyed my jests . . ."*

**21** FRIDAY

**22** SATURDAY    **23** SUNDAY

*St George's Day*

# *APRIL*

*A note says, "Need help – come quickly!"*
*Whatever can the matter be?*

**24** MONDAY

**25** TUESDAY

# APRIL

**26** WEDNESDAY

**27** THURSDAY

**28** FRIDAY

**29** SATURDAY          **30** SUNDAY

# *M A Y*

**1**  MONDAY

*Spring Bank Holiday (Scotland)*

**2**  TUESDAY

**3**  WEDNESDAY

**4**  THURSDAY

# MAY

*"Help!" calls Pong-Ping. "The door's shut tight!*
*The creeper's sprouted overnight!"*

**5**  FRIDAY

**6**  SATURDAY       **7**  SUNDAY

# MAY

*"We'll get you down!" cries Mr Bear.*
*"I'll fetch a ladder – just wait there . . . "*

**8**  MONDAY

*V.E. Day Celebration – Bank Holiday (UK)*

**9**  TUESDAY

# MAY

**10** WEDNESDAY

**11** THURSDAY

**12** FRIDAY

**13** SATURDAY      **14** SUNDAY

*Mothers' Day (Canada)*

# *M A Y*

**15** MONDAY

**16** TUESDAY

**17** WEDNESDAY

**18** THURSDAY

# MAY

*He trims the creeper. "Now you'll see –*
*It just needs pruning tidily!"*

**19** FRIDAY

**20** SATURDAY          **21** SUNDAY

# MAY

*"Look!" Pong-Ping cries. "It's back! What's more,*
*It's even thicker than before!"*

**22** MONDAY

*Victoria Day (Holiday, Canada)*

**23** TUESDAY

# M A Y

**24** WEDNESDAY

**25** THURSDAY

*Ascension Day*

**26** FRIDAY

**27** SATURDAY          **28** SUNDAY

**29** MONDAY

*Bank Holiday (UK)*

**30** TUESDAY

**31** WEDNESDAY

*Islamic New Year (1416)*

**1** THURSDAY

# JUNE

*"Take care!" says Mrs Bear. "I'll see
You later, when it's time for tea!"*

**2**  FRIDAY

**3**  SATURDAY  **4**  SUNDAY

*Whit Sunday – Pentecost*

# JUNE

*A court official's angered by*
*The way the Sage and Rupert fly!*

---

**5**   MONDAY

*Holiday (Rep. of Ireland)*

---

**6**   TUESDAY

# *J U N E*

**7** WEDNESDAY

**8** THURSDAY

**9** FRIDAY

**10** SATURDAY     **11** SUNDAY

*Trinity Sunday*

# JUNE

**12** MONDAY

**13** TUESDAY

**14** WEDNESDAY

**15** THURSDAY

# J U N E

*The Sage and Rupert both bow low.*
*The King hates aeroplanes, they know!*

---

**16**  FRIDAY

---

**17**  SATURDAY       **18**  SUNDAY

*Fathers' Day*

# JUNE

*"There!" Mrs Bear cries. "Look, you see,
I said they'd both be back for tea!"*

---

**19** MONDAY

---

**20** TUESDAY

# JUNE

**21** WEDNESDAY

*Summer begins – Longest Day*

**22** THURSDAY

**23** FRIDAY

**24** SATURDAY          **25** SUNDAY

*St Jean Baptiste (Holiday, Canada)*

# JUNE

**26** MONDAY

**27** TUESDAY

**28** WEDNESDAY

**29** THURSDAY

*Rupert and Bill are on their way*
*To start a boating holiday.*

**30** FRIDAY

**1** SATURDAY　　**2** SUNDAY

*Canada Day (Holiday, Canada)*

# JULY

*The motor boat goes racing past,*
*Then heads upstream, still travelling fast.*

**3**    MONDAY

**4**    TUESDAY

# *J U L Y*

**5**   WEDNESDAY

**6**   THURSDAY

**7**   FRIDAY

**8**   SATURDAY     **9**   SUNDAY

# JULY

**10**  MONDAY

**11**  TUESDAY

**12**  WEDNESDAY

*Bank Holiday (N. Ireland)*

**13**  THURSDAY

# JULY

*The willows hide something, he's sure,*
*So off they paddle, to explore . . .*

---

**14** FRIDAY

---

**15** SATURDAY

**16** SUNDAY

# JULY

*An old boathouse comes into view –*
*Algy and Bingo's boat's there too!*

---

**17**  MONDAY

---

**18**  TUESDAY

# J U L Y

**19** WEDNESDAY

**20** THURSDAY

**21** FRIDAY

**22** SATURDAY    **23** SUNDAY

# *J U L Y*

**24**  MONDAY

**25**  TUESDAY

**26**  WEDNESDAY

**27**  THURSDAY

# JULY

*"The motor boat!" gasps Bill. "Oh no!*
*If it's here then we'd better go!"*

---

**28**  FRIDAY

---

**29**  SATURDAY          **30**  SUNDAY

# JULY–AUGUST

*It's Rupert's summer holiday –*
*He's on his way to Rocky Bay . . .*

---

**31**  MONDAY

---

**1**  TUESDAY

# AUGUST

**2**    WEDNESDAY

**3**    THURSDAY

**4**    FRIDAY

**5**    SATURDAY      **6**    SUNDAY

# AUGUST

**7**  MONDAY

*Summer Bank Holiday (Scotland)*
*Holiday (Rep. of Ireland)*
*Civic Holiday (Canada)*

**8**  TUESDAY

**9**  WEDNESDAY

**10**  THURSDAY

# AUGUST

*The families meet on the beach.*
*"I've saved you all a deckchair each!"*

**11** FRIDAY

**12** SATURDAY      **13** SUNDAY

# AUGUST

*"Well done!" says Mr Bear. "Now you*
*Must join us for the picnic too."*

---

**14**  MONDAY

---

**15**  TUESDAY

# AUGUST

**16** WEDNESDAY

**17** THURSDAY

**18** FRIDAY

**19** SATURDAY          **20** SUNDAY

# AUGUST

**21** MONDAY

**22** TUESDAY

**23** WEDNESDAY

**24** THURSDAY

# AUGUST

*Then Mr Pig says, "Let's all play*
*A cricket match to end the day!"*

**25**  FRIDAY

**26**  SATURDAY          **27**  SUNDAY

# AUGUST

*"I've had a really lovely day!*
*I like it here at Rocky Bay . . . "*

---

**28** MONDAY

*Summer Bank Holiday (UK except Scotland)*

---

**29** TUESDAY

**30** WEDNESDAY

**31** THURSDAY

**1** FRIDAY

**2** SATURDAY      **3** SUNDAY

# *SEPTEMBER*

**4**   MONDAY

*Labour Day (Holiday, Canada)*

**5**   TUESDAY

**6**   WEDNESDAY

**7**   THURSDAY

# SEPTEMBER

*A music lesson starts the day –*
*"You sing," says Dr Chimp. "I'll play . . . "*

---

**8**  FRIDAY

---

**9**  SATURDAY          **10**  SUNDAY

# SEPTEMBER

*But Dr Chimp can't play for long,*
*"My goodness, all this music's wrong!"*

**11**  MONDAY

**12**  TUESDAY

# SEPTEMBER

**13** WEDNESDAY

**14** THURSDAY

**15** FRIDAY

**16** SATURDAY     **17** SUNDAY

# SEPTEMBER

**18** MONDAY

**19** TUESDAY

**20** WEDNESDAY

**21** THURSDAY

*The naughty Fox twins laugh with glee –
They've mixed it up deliberately!*

**22** FRIDAY

**23** SATURDAY      **24** SUNDAY

*Autumn begins*

# SEPTEMBER

*"Try it," he tells the pals. "If you
Catch one, you'll each get a wish too."*

---

**25** MONDAY

*Jewish New Year (5756) (Rosh Hashanah)*

---

**26** TUESDAY

**27** WEDNESDAY

**28** THURSDAY

**29** FRIDAY

**30** SATURDAY   **1** SUNDAY

# OCTOBER

**2** MONDAY

**3** TUESDAY

**4** WEDNESDAY

*Day of Atonement (Yom Kippur)*

**5** THURSDAY

# OCTOBER

*But Rupert's caught a note which pleads
For help. "H. E. L. P.!" he reads.*

**6**  FRIDAY

**7**  SATURDAY          **8**  SUNDAY

*Then Rupert cries, "I understand!
The note says that he wants to land!"*

**9** MONDAY

*Thanksgiving (Holiday, Canada)*

**10** TUESDAY

# OCTOBER

**11** WEDNESDAY

**12** THURSDAY

**13** FRIDAY

**14** SATURDAY
**15** SUNDAY

# OCTOBER

**16**  MONDAY

**17**  TUESDAY

**18**  WEDNESDAY

**19**  THURSDAY

# OCTOBER

*The chums hold tight, then realise*
*That the balloon's begun to rise.*

**20** FRIDAY

**21** SATURDAY

**22** SUNDAY

*A wind starts and the two pals find*
*They've soon left Nutwood far behind.*

**23** MONDAY

**24** TUESDAY

# OCTOBER

**25** WEDNESDAY

**26** THURSDAY

**27** FRIDAY

**28** SATURDAY    **29** SUNDAY

*British Summer Time ends*

**30** MONDAY

*Holiday (Rep. of Ireland)*

**31** TUESDAY

**1** WEDNESDAY

**2** THURSDAY

# NOVEMBER

*"A g..g..g..g..ghost!" cries Bill.*
*It seems the Manor's haunted still . . .*

**3** FRIDAY

**4** SATURDAY  **5** SUNDAY

*Then, as the pals look on in fear*
*They see the first ghost disappear!*

---

**6**   MONDAY

---

**7**   TUESDAY

# NOVEMBER

**8** WEDNESDAY

**9** THURSDAY

**10** FRIDAY

**11** SATURDAY      **12** SUNDAY

*Remembrance Day (Holiday, Canada)*      *Remembrance Sunday*

**13** MONDAY

**14** TUESDAY

**15** WEDNESDAY

**16** THURSDAY

# NOVEMBER

*Rupert and Ottoline fall through
The secret door and vanish too . . .*

**17** FRIDAY

**18** SATURDAY          **19** SUNDAY

*It's Freddy Fox! He's here as well*
*But hurt his ankle when he fell . . .*

**20** MONDAY

**21** TUESDAY

**22** WEDNESDAY

**23** THURSDAY

**24** FRIDAY

**25** SATURDAY     **26** SUNDAY

# NOVEMBER

**27** MONDAY

**28** TUESDAY

**29** WEDNESDAY

**30** THURSDAY

*St Andrew's Day*

# DECEMBER

*On Christmas Eve he waits all day*
*But there's no sign snow's on the way . . .*

---

**1**  FRIDAY

---

**2**  SATURDAY          **3**  SUNDAY

*First Sunday in Advent*

# DECEMBER

*The pair take off and quickly fly
To Santa's castle in the sky.*

---

**4**   MONDAY

---

**5**   TUESDAY

# DECEMBER

**6**  WEDNESDAY

**7**  THURSDAY

**8**  FRIDAY

**9**  SATURDAY      **10**  SUNDAY

# DECEMBER

**11** MONDAY

**12** TUESDAY

**13** WEDNESDAY

**14** THURSDAY

# DECEMBER

*It's warm in Santa's office too –*
*"This winter sun will never do!"*

---

**15**  FRIDAY

---

**16**  SATURDAY

**17**  SUNDAY

# DECEMBER

*"I need someone like you to go*
*And ask the Weather Clerk for snow."*

---

**18**  MONDAY

---

**19**  TUESDAY

# DECEMBER

**20** WEDNESDAY

**21** THURSDAY

**22** FRIDAY

*Winter begins – Shortest Day*

**23** SATURDAY      **24** SUNDAY

# DECEMBER

**25** MONDAY

*Christmas Day*

**26** TUESDAY

*Boxing Day (UK)*
*St Stephen's Day (Rep. of Ireland)*

**27** WEDNESDAY

**28** THURSDAY

# DECEMBER

*The Cowboy stays behind and tries*
*Out Rupert's sledge. "Yippee!" he cries.*

**29** FRIDAY

**30** SATURDAY    **31** SUNDAY